AF226112

The Mark of the Beast

An extraordinary look inside one of the most elusive but critical topics we all must know

Dispelling the Lies

A Terrifying Reality

Escaping the Mark

By Menachem Rae

ISBN: 978-1-7397271-0-9 (eBook)
ISBN: 978-1-7397271-1-6 (Paperback)
ISBN: 978-1-7397271-2-3 (Hardback)

Front cover image by Testifying of God Press
Book design by Testifying of God Press

First printing edition 2022.

Testifying of God Press

www.wakeuplookandsee.com

About The Author

Menachem Rae wants to take the backseat in life behind God. After taking part in the cage fight of life and seeing what it offers, resting in the bosom of someone who has power over it all is hugely comforting. Menachem took some time to commit fully to God, but with the strength of God and his messengers, standing boldly in the face of the world was possible.

Having looked at the state of the world and the downward trajectory, Menachem found it impossible to go along to get along. Understanding that to change a corrupt system from within would mean one has to be evil first to enter the system, thus defeating the original intention.

> **Something else is needed.**

This understanding meant the only viable alternative was siding with someone who desired and had the power to destroy the blight of this world.

Revelation 21:1-4 (KJV)

[1.] And I saw a new heaven and a new earth: for the first heaven and the first earth were passed away; and there was no more sea.

[2.] And I John saw the holy city, new Jerusalem, coming down from God out of heaven, prepared as a bride adorned for her husband.

[3.] And I heard a great voice out of heaven saying, Behold, the tabernacle of God is with men, and he will dwell with them, and they shall be his people, and God himself shall be with them, and be their God.

[4.] And God shall wipe away all tears from their eyes; and there shall be no more death, neither sorrow, nor crying, neither shall there be any more pain: for the former things are passed away.

Dedication

To God

If not for him, I would not be here today. He came for me when I was sinking in the mire and not knowing what was happening, and I am eternally grateful. I have dedicated my life to God—no turning back, and here, this book shows my gratitude.

John 6:37-40 (NIV)

37. All those the Father gives me will come to me, and whoever comes to me I will never drive away.

38. For I have come down from heaven not to do my will but to do the will of him who sent me.

39. And this is the will of him who sent me, that I shall lose none of all those he has given me, but raise them up at the last day.

40. For my Father's will is that everyone who looks to the Son and believes in him shall have eternal life, and I will raise them up at the last day.

How To Read This Book

The reader should read the entire book while putting a pin in the references to get to the conclusion and see the author's perspective. This approach enables a free flow of connecting thoughts without the stutter-stepping of checking references.

This approach is twofold, requiring a second pass of the book to check the author's references to get confirmation of the conclusion he draws and deeper insights into the foundational material.

The other approach would be to examine the book slowly while checking the references along the way. This approach will, of course, be more intense and might leave the uninitiated gasping for air as they navigate the information tree of a metaphorical Wikipedia rabbit hole, never to be seen again.

Or emerge like the phoenix rising from the ashes!

Both approaches are valid, and the underlying supporting information is essential. However, most people may find it an easier read first to intake the book and then dive deeper into the reference material. Others may find it necessary to establish each point on a foundation, rock, before moving on to the next.

Either way, the book is enjoyable and draws fascinating conclusions backed by evidence.

Where the author uses scriptural references, substituting another version is possible. Emphasise literal translations rather than translations that perform interpretations of the original text.

Most of the scriptural validation presented in this book is from the King James Version (KJV) of the protestant Bible but also used are the New International Version (NIV), English Standard Version (ESV), Revised Standard Version (RSV), Apocrypha, the Testaments of the Twelve Patriarchs, the Apocalypse of Paul and the Book of Jasher. It is vital to break the mental chains enacted by the institutions claiming to stand for God, but frankly, they are wolves in sheep's clothing.

The King James Version of the Bible may not be to everyone's taste, but frequently it has a more literal translation of the scriptures despite speaking in archaic British English. Suffer it so for now but use other versions to help navigate the grammar.

A Terrifying Reality
CONTENTS

1	The Stage
5	The Importance
10	A Kingdom Divided
13	Understanding Scriptures
25	Worship
33	Beast
39	Forehead
44	Right Hand
49	Buy or Sell
53	Name
58	The Number—666
69	The Sum
73	Guidance
82	The Final Word

Preface

The mark of the beast is one of the most popular topics today. It elicits both fear and intrigue while being a goldmine for Christian advocates and those who seek views and revenue in a highly monetised world.

Unfortunately, most authors on this topic have not come close to the truth but use fear and intrigue to hook their viewers or readers for personal gain.

2 Peter 2:1-3 (NIV)

---

[1] But there were also false prophets among the people, just as there will be false teachers among you. They will secretly introduce destructive heresies, even denying the sovereign Lord who bought them—bringing swift destruction on themselves.

[2] Many will follow their depraved conduct and will bring the way of truth into disrepute.

[3] In their greed, these teachers will exploit you with fabricated stories. Their condemnation has long

been hanging over them, and their destruction has not been sleeping.

So many people latch on to the current trends without little thought. Others who are genuinely searching get confused through the abundance of misinformation parading as truth. The scriptures[1] are a puzzle that only God can unlock, and only those who seek him with all their hearts will be privy to its understanding through him—a kingdom divided against itself cannot stand.

Matthew 12:25 (KJV)

And Jesus knew their thoughts, and said unto them, Every kingdom divided against itself is brought to desolation; and every city or house divided against itself shall not stand

Even more sinister, this world in which we temporarily live has an insidious group of people on every continent and nation, in every walk of life, who either through ignorance, greed, or both have attacked God and by association his servants, ferociously and relentlessly. They have left no stone unturned. They deliberately corrupt the understanding of the scriptures through countless avenues and pollute the world, strutting like peacocks walking against God's instructions, all to the end of personal gain and building their earthly kingdom.

But they counted our life a pastime, and our time here a market for gain: for, say they, we must be getting every way, though it be by evil means.

And through covetousness shall they with feigned words make merchandise of you: whose judgment now of a long time lingereth not, and their damnation slumbereth not.

Those who search for the meaning of life—God, without the King of Kings[2] could never navigate this miry maze. Even the deceivers themselves are deceived, but laugh, hands clasps or pointing to the sky, lording over the cattle with their well-kept signs and secrets.

This act is both on a level of dishonesty and deliberate deception, which deeply warrants correction.

> The chains taught to you which hold you in place
> must break to move forward.

Acknowledgements

I want to thank my wonderful wife for standing by my side through the entire journey, moving away from the world to God. Without her support, it would have been much harder to complete this book, and I am eternally grateful for her help reading my drafts and playing her role in our wonderful family.

I want to thank God for coming for me and showing me that there is more than this world. Without that experience and his constant support, I can guarantee that I would not have made it this far. The journey is not over, but I have seen the

evidence that he will stand beside me, and all that
is left is for me to do my part.

Chapter 1
The Stage

ew other topics are as divisive as the "the mark of the beast". It causes fear, panic, curiosity, fascination, and a raft of other emotions that create a cocktail ripe for deception, control, and monetisation of the many faces of people around the world.

The following passage started the explosion of widespread conversation within every nation, people, race, and religion on earth.

Revelation 13:16-18 (KJV)

16. And he causeth all, both small and great, rich and poor, free and bond, to receive a mark in their **right hand**, or in their **foreheads**:

The Mark of the Beast

[17] And that no man might **buy or sell**, save he that had the **mark**, or the **name of the beast**, or the **number of his name**.

[18] Here is wisdom. Let him that hath understanding count the number of the beast: for it is the number of a man; and his number *is* **Six hundred threescore** *and* **six**.

The "beast" causes everyone to receive a mark in their right hand or forehead. Without this mark, the name, or the number of this beast, no one will be able to buy or sell.

This book deciphers this passage and maps it to the world, using the scriptures as its underpinning foundation.

> ### What is absolute truth?
>
> ### Where do you find the absolute truth?
>
> There must be a benchmark, a measuring rod to weigh against when examining data to determine correct and incorrect.
>
> Since the scriptures speak of the mark of the beast, then what else must provide understanding to validate the writing? No one can apply any other measure since this would take liberties and make assumptions about the author's intent.

The premise held from cover to cover is that scripture explains scripture and unlocks the overall puzzle when the understanding is combined. The scriptures tell us this is the case in Isaiah 28:9-10[3].

Most of the audience finds themselves in an unenviable dilemma in that their understanding of the scriptures is limited or non-existent. Because of this, they make assumptions and decisions from a position of ignorance.

The average person does not consider where they get their knowledge. They take for granted that the sources of so-called information established in their eyes from their births are valid, precise, objective, and have their best interests at heart. The **Stage** requires that the reader examine their truth, what they know, and how they got that knowledge.

The simple act of choosing to read this book shows initiative and willingness to work, taking the lead rather than allowing others to lead you like an ox to the stocks.

Despite the relentless assault on the validity of the scriptures in the world today, this book will show compelling secrets hidden that will blow your mind and establish that the scriptures, a literary masterpiece written thousands of years ago through God's inspiration, is as valid today as ever.

> **TIP: Check out How To Read This Book.**

Chapter 2

The Importance

Knowing the Mark of the Beast is of utmost importance because of the consequences (Revelation 14:9-11[4], 16:2[5]; 19:20[6]; 20:4[7]) and the rewards (James 1:12[8], Matthew 25:21[9], Revelation 22:12[10], Jeremiah 17:9-10[11]) outlined in the scriptures.

Because of this, the wicked have exploited it for confusion, power, and personal gain. The architects corral the people as livestock into states of confusion where they daily fight to find the truth. The truth is there to set them free from the chains of this world, but first, you must find it and second, you must endure the journey.

Revelation 14:9-11 (KJV)

The Mark of the Beast

---

[9] And the third angel followed them, saying with a loud voice, If any man worship the beast and his image, and receive his mark in his forehead, or in his hand,

[10] The same shall drink of the wine of the wrath of God, which is poured out without mixture into the cup of his indignation; and he shall be tormented with fire and brimstone in the presence of the holy angels, and in the presence of the Lamb:

[11] And the smoke of their torment ascendeth up for ever and ever: and they have no rest day nor night, who worship the beast and his image, and whosoever receiveth the mark of his name.

The mark of the beast is said to be many things:

- COVID-19 vaccines
- Vaccination passports
- Emperor Caesar Nero
- The Sunday Sabbath (Referred to as worship)
- RFID chip implant
- Biometric ID Card
- Tattooed barcode
- Genetically modified/engineered humans
- A combination of letters and symbols placed on your forehead or right hand
- Facebook data collection
- World payment system

- Nationalism and following the world political system
- One world religion
- Cashless society
- Emperor Nero (Neron Kaiser)
- National ID card
- Schemes of Bill Gates
- Firebrand
- Electrical power
- UPC Code
- Bitcoin
- One world currency
- CERN
- M. K. ULTRA
- Plus, many more

The masses flock to these wild deceptions because of the spark of incredible that surrounds them and the divisive nature they exhibit. Not to mention, these wild ideas are spread with a vengeance in all media outlets, large and small, mainstream and non-mainstream. Most people also love these answers because it gives them a simple solution that doesn't require them to change their lives beyond the superficial, if at all.

We live in a world where people are treated as merchandise (2 Peter 2:1-3[12], Wisdom of Solomon 15:12[13]), using divisive tactics to keep them blind while manufacturing every conceivable avenue to sell

The Mark of the Beast

them another product and monetise their entire existence. The purpose, in this case, is to distract the people from the heart of the matter, spending their time chasing fanciful incantations. This detour leaves them deceived, tired, discouraged, confused, submissive, obsessed, and in their final death throes, they give in to the open arms of religion (including atheism), materialism, and the chains of the world.

> Not only are the masses deceived, but the deceivers also are handed carrots where they believe the illusions that they are the architects; however, they also are noosed and are the walking dead. One cannot work in darkness to serve the true light[14].

Both in religion and the other systems of the world, you will spend a lot of time memorising doctrines, either through their literature, schools, universities, media, and many outlets, including the almighty television—one of the greatest transmissions of filth and deception ever invented.

To understand the mark of the beast, you must understand all the following, with the most critical being worship and what it is. Worship is far different from what is masqueraded today in the entertainment and brainwashing centres called churches, mosques, temples and synagogues. As so often happens, the foundation of our knowledge is sand rather than a rock.

1. **Worship**
2. **Beast**
3. Mark in the **Forehead**
4. Mark in the **Right Hand**
5. **Name** of the Beast
6. **Number** of the Beast (**666**)
7. To **Buy** or **Sell**

To avoid receiving the mark, you must know what it is, appreciate the severity of the situation, and be prepared to act in your life despite your fears and difficulties.

Chapter 3

A Kingdom Divided

The subtle flood of teachings the world has spewed will make this chapter hard to swallow. There is a point in each of our lives where we must face the truth; explaining things away or rejecting new information just will not cut it. Let's hope today is the day.

The scriptures are fascinating on many levels. One level is where it is only possible to understand it if the author gives that knowledge to you[15]. Only when you search for Him, shown by the evidence of following his instructions, will He give you "wisdom" to understand. No man empowers the enemy to fight against himself, even the Most High (Mark 3:24[16]).

Job 28:28 (KJV)

And unto man he said, Behold, the fear of the Lord, that is wisdom; and to depart from evil is understanding.

The scriptures are written for those who seek God (Matthew 13:10-11[17]) and cannot be deciphered without the help of God. His thoughts are far beyond our understanding (Isaiah 55:8-9[18]). To seek God is the most critical thing you can do, even beyond the acquisition of riches (Proverbs 16:16[19], Ecclesiastes 12:13-14[20]).

The world's wisdom, science & technology, and the quest for the holy grail, Avalon[21], or the fountain of youth through their power is foolishness (1 Corinthians 3:19[22]), not just in its inaccuracy or incompleteness but also in its sheer attempt to create a world without God and to explain Him away.

The poles of this division between those who serve the world or God are far apart, and nobody can be a member of the two sides. An evil branch cannot produce good fruits, and thus nobody who does the work of the devil can be on the side of God—no exceptions or excuses.

From conception into this world, there is an onslaught (Revelation 12:4[23]) for the destruction of our very soul—breaking it away from God. The attack is conducted with skill beyond measure, outside of God (2 Esdras 16:75[24]), you will ever encounter in

The Mark of the Beast

your life. It is a constant bombardment of deception established for centuries that you alone cannot navigate, and anyone who thinks they can is sorely deluded, simply showing that they are unaware of the deception.

> The waters are so rough that it takes someone who knows the way and is a master navigator to get through this journey.

Chapter 4

Understanding Scriptures

The scriptures have a lot of information. Many parts are written in prophetic language, indecipherable without knowing the precepts and how to approach the scriptures.

One of the critical concepts of the layout of the scriptures builds on the understanding that meanings are not necessarily reliant on today's definition but found inside the scriptures. This structure means the scriptures define the words and phrases it uses within itself. Here are a few examples to give you an understanding.

Examples:

STOCK

Definition Today	**noun** - the goods or merchandise kept on the premises of a shop or warehouse and available for sale or distribution. - the capital raised by a company or corporation through the issue and subscription of shares. - liquid made by cooking bones, meat, fish, or vegetables slowly in water, used as a basis for the preparation of soup, gravy, or sauces. - a person's ancestry or line of descent. - the trunk or woody stem of a living tree or shrub, especially one into which a graft (scion) is inserted. - a herbaceous European plant that is cultivated for its fragrant lilac, pink, or white flowers. - **HISTORICAL:** an instrument of punishment consisting of an adjustable wooden structure with holes for securing a person's feet and hands, in which criminals were

locked and exposed to public ridicule or assault.
- the part of a rifle or other firearm to which the barrel and firing mechanism are attached, held against one's shoulder when firing the gun.
- a band of white material tied like a cravat and worn as a part of formal horse-riding dress.
- a frame used to support a ship or boat out of water, especially when under construction.

adjective

- (of a product or type of product) usually kept in stock and thus regularly available for sale.
- (of a phrase or expression) so regularly used as to be automatic or hackneyed.

verb

- have or keep a supply of (a particular product or type or product) available for sale.
- fit (a rifle or other firearm)

	with a stock.
Etymology	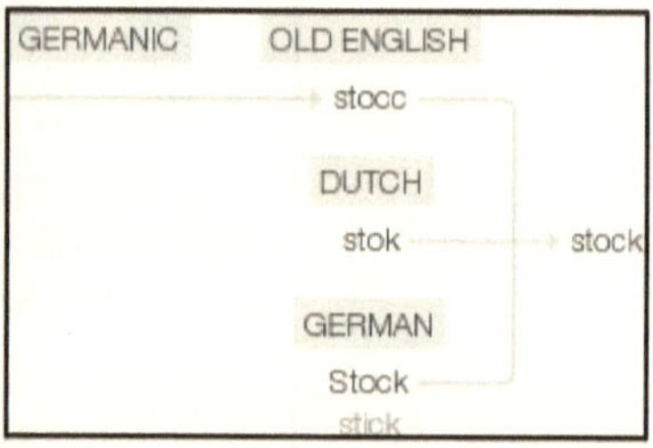 Old English *stoc(c)* **'trunk, block of wood, post'**, of Germanic origin; related to Dutch *stok* and German *Stock* 'stick'. The notion 'store, fund' (stock (sense 1 of the noun and sense 2 of the noun)) arose in late Middle English and is of obscure origin, perhaps expressing 'growth from a central stem' or 'firm foundation'.
Biblical Statement	And it came to pass through the lightness of her whoredom, that she defiled the land, and committed adultery with stones and with **stocks**. Jeremiah 3:9[25]
Typical Understanding	The worshipping of wood and stones when using the historical definition of stock for that time period.

Precept Definition of Stock	But they are altogether brutish and foolish: **the stock *is* a doctrine of vanities**. Jeremiah 10:8[26]
Precept Definition of Vanity	I have seen all the works that are done under the sun; and, behold, **all *is* vanity and vexation of spirit**. Ecclesiastes 1:14[27] The entire book of Ecclesiastes explains vanity in biblical precept terms.
What is not Vanity	Let us hear the conclusion of the whole matter: **Fear God, and keep his commandments**: for this *is* the whole *duty* of man. Ecclesiastes 12:13[28]
Biblical Understanding	The city/people (her precept) didn't keep the commandments of God, showing no respect for God but rather valuing and teaching the love of material possessions and other things contrary to God.

WATERS	
Biblical Statement	[1] Cast thy bread upon the waters: for thou shalt find it after many days. [2] Give a portion to seven, and also to eight; for thou knowest not what evil shall be upon the earth. Ecclesiastes 11:1-2[29]
Definition of Waters	And he saith unto me, **The waters which thou sawest, where the whore sitteth, are peoples, and multitudes, and nations, and tongues**. Revelation 17:15[30]
Definition of Bread	Remove far from me vanity and lies: give me neither poverty nor riches; feed me with food convenient for me: Proverbs 30:8[31] Behold, the days come, saith the Lord GOD, that I will send a famine in the land, not a famine of bread, nor a thirst for water, but of hearing the words of the LORD: Amos 8:11[32]

Biblical Understanding	Cast what you have, including the word of God, upon the people, and your rewards will be returned to you in time. Whereas bread can mean food, it can also mean other things needed in life and what can nourish or sustain you, and most importantly, the Word of God.

SEAS	
Biblical Statement	Therefore rejoice, *ye* heavens, and ye that dwell in them. Woe to the inhabiters of the earth and of the **sea**! for the devil is come down unto you, having great wrath, because he knoweth that he hath but a short time. Revelation 12:12[33]
Definition of Sea	And God called the dry *land* Earth; **and the gathering together of the waters called he Seas**: and God saw that *it was* good.

The Mark of the Beast

	Genesis 1:10[34]
Biblical Understanding	The peoples and nations (waters precept) of the earth (seas precept) are in big trouble because of the devil's wrath. He has a short time, so he acts fast and ferociously.

On one level, the scriptures show a sequence of events while plotting a world map on another. It testifies of Jesus and maps the historical tribes and nations to today. It provides information on the luminary (sun, moon and stars) calendar and many pieces of the puzzle to solve many things, including prophecies.

> **The hands of time cannot change what is built on this rock[35].**

Many well-learned individuals spend a lot of time developing encryption algorithms to secure data; however, these algorithms always get broken. On the other hand, the inspired written word of God is a *literary masterpiece* that has lasted for centuries, with the only ones able to decipher it being those with "wisdom" given by God. To everyone else, the words appear as foolishness.

Anyone who has tried to access the superficial and, much more so, the deeper secrets would understand just what I mean. The mysteries are such that some people will not even realise there is something to be accessed. It's a work of words encrypted for thousands of years from billions of eyes. God has inspired[36] all scriptures and ensured that only those sincerely searching for Him will find Him.

> **These are the only people worthy of Him.**

Matthew 13:10-17 (KJV)

[10.] And the disciples came, and said unto him, Why speakest thou unto them in parables?

[11.] He answered and said unto them, **Because it is given unto you to know the mysteries of the kingdom of heaven**, but to them it is not given.

[12.] For whosoever hath, to him shall be given, and he shall have more abundance: but whosoever hath not, from him shall be taken away even that he hath.

[13.] Therefore speak I to them in parables: because they seeing see not; and hearing they hear not, neither do they understand.

[14.] And in them is fulfilled the prophecy of Esaias[37], which saith, By hearing ye shall hear, and shall not understand; and seeing ye shall see, and shall not perceive:

The Mark of the Beast

15. For this people's heart is waxed gross, and *their* ears are dull of hearing, and their eyes they have closed; lest at any time they should see with *their* eyes, and hear with *their* ears, and should understand with *their* heart, and should be converted, and I should heal them.

16. But blessed *are* your eyes, for they see: and your ears, for they hear.

17. For verily I say unto you, That many prophets and righteous *men* have desired to see *those things* which ye see, and have not seen *them*; and to hear *those things* which ye hear, and have not heard *them*.

Indeed, you must know scripture personally to understand anything in scripture. Seek God by studying what he has given us, thinking on his words, meeting him in communication; otherwise, just sitting around expecting revelations would tempt him, which is a sin (Matthew 4:3-7[38]). To receive anything in scriptures requires a genuine desire for God, followed by action. Unless you act, you will receive nothing. Only those with wisdom (Proverbs 9:8-10[39]) will understand.

While I'm not too fond of biblical prescriptions, still, I will provide a few things I deem required to get on track to understanding scriptures:

- Join the side of God—God's kingdom (A kingdom divided against itself will surely fall[40]). Joining God's side is done by searching out, committing in your heart and keeping his instructions—commandments, as you learn.

- Pray to God for wisdom (precept) which only comes if God gives[41] it.

- Search for God with all your heart—appreciate the power and scope of God and humble yourself.

- Study the scriptures daily and pace yourself. Living by the instructions must be your entire world while remembering that pure religion[42] is not the same as religion today.

- Meditate on the things of God—think about his word and the mysteries.

- Build line upon line and precept upon precept[43] and appreciate that the scriptures act as its dictionary—each line has a life of its own, but they have a more remarkable life together.

- Appreciate there are many layers to the scriptures and that it teaches many things.

- Understand that God teaches his servants; therefore, humble yourself and submit to His will[44]. Teaching comes not only from reading the scriptures but also in your daily life. The path to life is walked by you and navigated by God through his Son.

The Mark of the Beast

- Perseverance. Please do not give up despite the difficulty.

Chapter 5

Worship

What exactly is worship?

How do we worship God?

Is it bowing down and prostrating yourself, or is it singing worship songs with your hands raised in the air? What about marching around a rock many times or bowing in front of a wall again and again? Maybe it's speaking ritualistic words and performing rituals on specific days? Is it going to church, the mosque, temple or synagogue and taking part in the service of the day? Is it the feeling or expression of reverence and adoration for a deity?

Is it an act of religious devotion, where religion is "the belief in and worship of a superhuman controlling power, especially a personal God or gods"?

Did you notice the circular logic where worship is in terms of religion and religion defined in terms of worship? An Ouroboros where logic consumes itself, and in the end, there is nothing.

Better yet, is it anything you do that declares the worth of the Lord, which deepens your relationship with Jesus and urges others to follow him? Is it the priority of who God is in our lives and where God is on our list of priorities?

To get to the bottom of this, we must use the scriptures to explain itself.

The name of Jesus has been misused and tarnished to the degree that many people have an aversion when they hear the word, whether they will admit it. Still, this example is vital to understanding worship and unlocking the truth.

Revelation 19:10 (KJV)

And I fell at his feet to worship him. And he said unto me, See *thou do it* not: I am thy fellowservant, and of thy brethren that have the testimony of Jesus: **worship God**: for the testimony of Jesus is the spirit of prophecy.

Revelation 19:10[45] highlights one of the critical roles that Jesus played on earth, his testimony, presenting evidence of worshipping God. One definition of worship even went as far as worshipping Jesus, when Jesus himself gave evidence of God. However, we did not see Jesus worship in the ways listed above except for putting God first, but not as we imagine it today, but in terms of how God requires it.

Paul explains in the language where he differentiates between the body (flesh) and the Spirit (Romans 8:8-9[46]).

Romans 8:8-9 (KJV)

---

8. So then they that are in the flesh cannot please God.

9. But ye are not in the flesh, but in the Spirit, if so be that the Spirit of God dwell in you. Now if any man have not the Spirit of Christ, he is none of his.

God requires worship in the Spirit, but what does that mean?

This Spirit that he refers to comes from God, which dwells in everyone; each person has their share of God. This statement is not to imply that we are gods or have access to the power of ascended masters, as the I AM movement claims, but to say that the Spirit of God is in all of us.

The Mark of the Beast

There is significant confusion here as the term "Spirit" is used in context with Jesus, the comforter, the Holy Spirit, the Spirit of God, and wisdom (precept).

In early Christian writing, The Apocalypse of Paul, Paul clarifies which spirit he is speaking of in Romans, in the New Testament.

Excerpt from Chapter 14, The Apocalypse of Paul (The receiving into heaven the soul of a righteous man)

Do manfully, for thou hast done the will of God while placed in the earth. And there came to meet him the angel who watched him every day, and said to him: Do manfully, soul; for I rejoice in thee, because thou hast done the will of God on earth: for I related to God all thy works, such as they were. Similarly also the **spirit** proceeded to meet him and said: Soul, fear not, nor be disturbed, until thou comest into a place which thou hast never known, but I will be a helper unto thee: for I found in thee a place of refreshment in the time when I dwelt in thee, while I was on earth. And his **spirit** strengthened him, and his angel received him, and led him into heaven: and an angel said: Whither runnest thou, O soul, and dost thou dare to enter into heaven? Wait and let us see if there is anything of ours in thee: and behold we find nothing in thee. I see also thy divine helper and angel, and the spirit is rejoicing along with thee, because thou hast done the will of God on earth.

You, the person, are the soul, an individual with a mind and free will between those two poles: the Body and the Spirit.

Each one tugs at us, but we have the option of choosing whose call we welcome. To worship God in the Spirit, we must listen to His Spirit and follow His instructions.

The Mark of the Beast

Sin & the Body

Established in the people's hearts are the sins of this earth. The man of sin sits in the temple of God as if he were God (2 Thessalonians 2:1-10[48]). Wickedness is prevalent and is pushed with an unceasing vengeance on us every day. Without the Spirit of God, which he has given to us, none of us could escape this onslaught.

Sadly, most people have embraced the flesh and chased after the things of this world, and thus the Spirit does not influence them—they have chosen their side.

The Temple

The body is the temple of God (1 Corinthians 3:16-17[49], 1 Corinthians 6:15-20[50]). We should rejoice in the destruction of the physical sanctuary (Matthew 24:2[51], John 4:21-23[52]) since God has removed those remnants of the need for men on earth to intercede for us.

Ezekiel 44:7[53] and Ezekiel 44:9[54] show God's importance on keeping our bodies undefiled, where being defiled is breaking his instructions.

The Testimony

Every instruction written in the scriptures for Jesus to accomplish was fulfilled (Luke 24:44[55]) by him.

This example set for us highlights we must do the same. Therefore, by keeping our soul clean, by doing the will of God, we indeed worship God in the Spirit.

Worship

To listen to the Spirit is to listen to God and follow his instructions. The Spirit, as did Jesus, testifies of God.

Jesus never prostrated himself and performed many antics in the name of worship. He didn't dwell on "worship songs", which cleverly and subtly attempt to redefine worship. Jesus also never defined "good" in his terms since there is only one good, and that is God (Luke 18:19[56]). We must do good, but according to God's definition of good, that is to follow his instructions by his word instead of someone else coming in their name[57].

John 14:13-15 (KJV)

---

[13] And whatsoever ye shall ask in my name, that will I do, that the Father may be glorified in the Son.

[14] If ye shall ask any thing in my name, I will do it.

[15] If ye love me, keep my commandments.

---

1 John 5:3 (KJV)

For this is the love of God, that we keep his commandments: and his commandments are not grievous.

To worship God is to do God's will and thus, to worship anything is to do the will of that thing. Worshipping Satan is to do his will, to honour yourself is to do your own will (if that's possible since our identity is defined as either for God or against Him), and to worship anyone is to do their will. If we do the will of this world, then we are indeed worshipping this world.

Chapter 6

Daniel 2:31-45 (KJV)

---

31. Thou, O king, sawest, and behold a great image. This great image, whose brightness was excellent, stood before thee; and the form thereof was terrible.

32. This image's head was of fine gold, his breast and his arms of silver, his belly and his thighs of brass,

33. His legs of iron, his feet part of iron and part of clay.

34. Thou sawest till that a stone was cut out without hands, which smote the image upon his feet that were of iron and clay, and brake them to pieces.

35. Then was the iron, the clay, the brass, the silver, and the gold, broken to pieces together, and became like the chaff of the summer threshingfloors; and the wind carried them away, that no place was found for them: and the stone that smote the image became a great mountain, and filled the whole earth.

36. This is the dream; and we will tell the interpretation thereof before the king.

37. Thou, O king, art a king of kings: for the God of heaven hath given thee a kingdom, power, and strength, and glory.

38. And wheresoever the children of men dwell, the beasts of the field and the fowls of the heaven hath he given into thine hand, and hath made thee ruler over them all. Thou art this head of gold.

39. And after thee shall arise another kingdom inferior to thee, and another third kingdom of brass, which shall bear rule over all the earth.

40. And the fourth kingdom shall be strong as iron: forasmuch as iron breaketh in pieces and subdueth all things: and as iron that breaketh all these, shall it break in pieces and bruise.

41. And whereas thou sawest the feet and toes, part of potters' clay, and part of iron, the kingdom shall be divided; but there shall be in it of the strength of the iron, forasmuch as thou sawest the iron mixed with miry clay.

[42] And as the toes of the feet were part of iron, and part of clay, so the kingdom shall be partly strong, and partly broken.

[43] And whereas thou sawest iron mixed with miry clay, they shall mingle themselves with the seed of men: but they shall not cleave one to another, even as iron is not mixed with clay.

[44] And in the days of these kings shall the God of heaven set up a kingdom, which shall never be destroyed: and the kingdom shall not be left to other people, but it shall break in pieces and consume all these kingdoms, and it shall stand for ever.

[45] Forasmuch as thou sawest that the stone was cut out of the mountain without hands, and that it brake in pieces the iron, the brass, the clay, the silver, and the gold; the great God hath made known to the king what shall come to pass hereafter: and the dream is certain, and the interpretation thereof sure.

Daniel interprets Nebuchadnezzar's dream through God's revelations and analyses the image divided into gold, silver, brass, iron plus iron and clay. Throughout the interpretation of Nebuchadnezzar's dream, Daniel refers to the different metals as kingdoms or dominions.

Daniel 2:39 (KJV)

And after thee shall arise another kingdom inferior to thee, and another third kingdom of brass, which shall bear rule over all the earth.

This word kingdom is מַלְכוּ (**malku**) in the Aramaic language, meaning **dominion,** which is a **realm, royalty** or **reign**, indicating that a kingdom is a rule (physical or otherwise), but not fixed to a landmass.

The subsequent passages describe the fourth beast as the fourth kingdom.

Daniel 7:3 (KJV)

And four great beasts came up from the sea, diverse one from another.

Daniel 7:23 (KJV)

Thus he said, The fourth beast shall be the fourth kingdom upon earth, which shall be diverse from all kingdoms, and shall devour the whole earth, and shall tread it down, and break it in pieces.

This correlation highlights a beast is a kingdom, a dominion of some sort. This beast, the kingdom of iron shown in Nebuchadnezzar's dream, essentially has authority or control over the entire earth.

NOTE: The fourth beast devours the whole earth and treads (to trample, Aramaic דּוּשׁ) it down. The understanding that immediately comes to mind is breaking it down underfoot, which could be wars, for example. However, the word tread is equal to the etymological meaning of the word <u>trade</u> (examined further in the chapter on <u>buy or sell</u>).

Treading down the earth is saying to destroy the earth, turning it against God for and through monetary gain using occupation (jobs), financial structures, business, greed and the measuring stick of economic growth and self-interest for everything. The quest for profit results in the work-life enslavement of the people, using financial structures such as inflation to keep prices rising, successfully attempting the bondage of everyone and the destruction of the world.

Furthermore:

Revelation 19:19-20 (KJV)

19. And I saw the beast, and the kings of the earth, and their armies, gathered together to make war against him that sat on the horse, and against his army.

20. And the beast was taken, and with him the false prophet that wrought miracles before him, with which he deceived them that had received the mark of the beast, and them that worshipped his image.

The Mark of the Beast

These both were cast alive into a lake of fire
burning with brimstone.

This passage further highlights that a beast is a
dominion, made up of the kings of the earth—the
leaders of the world and their armies. Note that this
beast spans multiple kings—the kingdom includes
many nations or dominions. So, a beast is not limited
to a single country, nation, government, or tribe but
can span many of these entities and represent a
"rulership". It means the world.

> **SIDE NOTE:** It seems nothing will deter the beast
> despite knowing the outcome of the war with God;
> they will lose even though they will enjoy the things
> of the earth now. God's servants will suffer as a
> testament against their persecutors[58] but receive
> their reward later.

Chapter 7

Forehead

18. Therefore shall ye lay up these my words in your heart and in your soul, and bind them for a sign upon your hand, that they may be as **frontlets between your eyes**.

19. And ye shall teach them your children, speaking of them when thou sittest in thine house, and when thou walkest by the way, when thou liest down, and when thou risest up.

Moses read the laws of God to the Israelites in Deuteronomy, and he commanded they should keep or lay up the words in their hearts and minds (frontlets between their eyes). To both live by the instructions and teach them to the next generations.

The Mark of the Beast

In this one passage, the forehead is explained, but a single piece of evidence is hardly enough to draw a conclusion. Luckily, the evidence is literally littered throughout the scriptures.

Deuteronomy 6:6-8 (KJV)

6. And these words, which I command thee this day, shall be in thine heart:

7. And thou shalt teach them diligently unto thy children, and shalt talk of them when thou sittest in thine house, and when thou walkest by the way, and when thou liest down, and when thou risest up.

8. And thou shalt bind them for a sign upon thine hand, and they shall be as **frontlets between thine eyes**.

Exodus 13:9 (KJV)

And it shall be for a sign unto thee upon thine hand, and for a memorial **between thine eyes**, that the LORD's law may be in thy mouth: for with a strong hand hath the LORD brought thee out of Egypt.

Hebrews 10:16 (KJV)

This is the covenant that I will make with them after those days, saith the Lord, I will put my laws into their hearts, **and in their minds will I write them;**

Luke 6:45[59] shows that the heart refers to the mind when used in specific contexts. The soul (individual) is represented by the principles someone lives by and what guides their life; the body or flesh is a host for the mind. What we speak is what we hold in our mind (our heart), especially the things we hold dear. Our passion may be our job, pastimes, kids, money, house, assets, business, sex, hedonism, gossip, theft, vulgarity, scheming, adultery, love, kindness, etc.

Luke 6:45 (KJV)

A good man out of the good treasure of his heart bringeth forth that which is good; and an evil man out of the evil treasure of his heart bringeth forth that which is evil: for of the abundance of the heart his mouth speaketh.

Bind the instructions in the forehead

Learn them, do them, keep them close to your heart (mind, remembrance, principles, and passion), and teach them to the next generations.

Whatever is in your heart will be in your conversation and actions.

Matthew 19:17 (KJV)

And he said unto him, Why callest thou me good? there is none good but one, that is, God: but if thou wilt enter into life, keep the commandments.

Good things are those things of God since there is only one good. We are to bind things that are good in our hearts—our minds, live by them and teach them to our children. The world redefines the word **"good"**, but Jesus clarified that there is none other good besides God. We must weigh everything against this measuring stick; otherwise, we are in a state of "relativity"—where each person has their personal definition of right and wrong.

Jesus's doctrine only we must follow since he came in the name of the Father, and through him, the Father does the work; thus, Jesus's instructions are God's instructions.

The forehead is our mind, which represents us as individuals—souls. Our identity is shaped by what we mentally consume and speak with our mouths. These become the acts of what we teach and the philosophies we live by.

Chapter 8

Right Hand

This chapter continues with the theme of using the scripture to answer the questions of scripture. The passages show the usage of hand or right hand and the common understanding of scripture.

Exodus 6:1 (KJV)

Then the LORD said unto Moses, Now shalt thou see what I will do to Pharaoh: for with **a strong hand** shall he let them go, and with **a strong hand** shall he drive them out of his land.

Genesis 31:29 (KJV)

It is in the power of my **hand** to do you hurt: but the God of your father spake unto me yesternight, saying, Take thou heed that thou speak not to Jacob either good or bad.

Thy right hand, O LORD, is become glorious in power: thy **right hand**, O LORD, hath dashed in pieces the enemy.

From these verses, we can deduce that the hand or right hand represents someone's power, the actions they can take, achieve, or the things they do. The scriptures provide many examples of this understanding, including the following.

And thou say in thine heart, My power and the might of mine **hand** hath gotten me this wealth.

Both riches and honour come of thee, and thou reignest over all; and in thine hand is power and might; and in thine **hand** it is to make great, and to give strength unto all.

And under their **hand** was an army, three hundred thousand and seven thousand and five hundred, that

The Mark of the Beast

made war with mighty power, to help the king against the enemy.

These examples again show the act of doing or achieving something through the power you possess, whether through your physical strength or the capabilities you have by other means, represents your hand or right hand. Combining this with the mark of the beast, we need to consider the following verse.

Luke 6:45 (KJV)

A good man out of the good treasure of his heart bringeth forth that which is good; and an evil man out of the evil treasure of his heart bringeth forth that which is evil: for of the abundance of the heart his mouth speaketh.

When we use our power in opposition to the good things of God, his instructions, we, therefore, have the mark on our right hand. We are working for the enemy of God and the kingdom that does not worship God.

Deuteronomy 11:18-19 (KJV)

18. Therefore shall ye lay up these my words in your heart and in your soul, and bind them for a sign upon your **hand**, that they may be as frontlets between your eyes.

¹⁹· And ye shall teach them your children, speaking of them when thou sittest in thine house, and when thou walkest by the way, when thou liest down, and when thou risest up.

Deuteronomy 6:6-8 (KJV)

---

⁶· And these words, which I command thee this day, shall be in thine heart:

⁷· And thou shalt teach them diligently unto thy children, and shalt talk of them when thou sittest in thine house, and when thou walkest by the way, and when thou liest down, and when thou risest up.

⁸· And thou shalt bind them for a sign upon thine **hand**, and they shall be as frontlets between thine eyes.

Exodus 13:9 (KJV)

And it shall be for a sign unto thee upon thine **hand**, and for a memorial between thine eyes, that the LORD's law may be in thy mouth.

Another way of looking at the "right hand" can be your acts or deeds: the things you do and produce. This product can be the actions themselves or how others receive and exhibit your activities.

Psalm 77:10-12 (KJV)

---

10. And I said, This is my infirmity: but I will remember the years of the **right hand** of the most High.

11. I will remember the **works** of the LORD: surely I will remember thy wonders of old.

12. I will meditate also of all thy **work**, and talk of thy doings.

Matthew 7:16 (KJV)

Ye shall know them by their fruits. Do men gather grapes of thorns, or figs of thistles?

> The only way to answer the question is by using the scriptures to provide evidence of what it stated. What we do reflects who we are.

Book of Jasher 34:68

And with thy **strong hand** and outstretched arm deliver my sons and their servants from them, for power and might are in **thy hands** to do all this.

> **Your right hand equals your works or actions through the power you possess. These works can either be good or evil, where God defines good and bad goes against God.**

Chapter 9
Buy or Sell

Not being able to buy or sell is likened to various things, all with the theme of controlling someone's access to their money and how they spend it. Like everything around this topic, the mill is in overdrive about what it means and could be.

- Credit cards
- Barcode tagging
- Microchip implants
- etc

This access control to someone's money is central to the term buy or sell, but the themes above do not hit the mark.

Another way of looking at the term is business, businessman, trading, trader, or **trade**.

Trade

Trade is defined as ***"the action of buying and selling goods and services"***. When we examine the etymology of the word, we get:

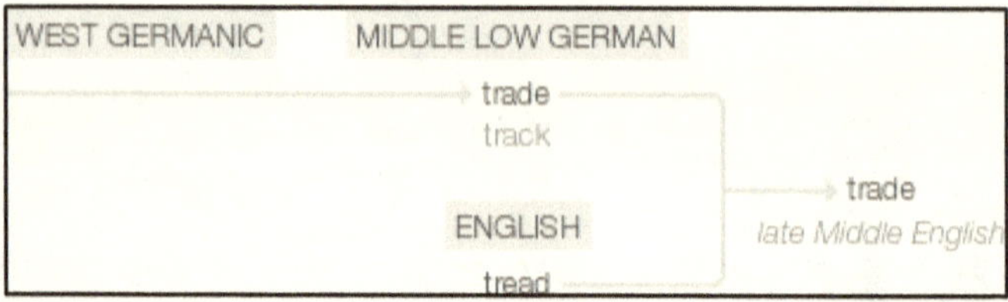

Late Middle English (as a noun): from Middle Low German, literally 'track', of West Germanic origin; related to tread. Early senses included 'course, way of life', which gave rise in the 16th century to 'habitual practice of an occupation', 'skilled handicraft'. The current verb senses date from the late 16th century.

The etymology reveals the origins of the word meant:

- Course, showing the route or direction followed by something/someone
- Way of life
- Habitual practice of an occupation
- Skilled handicraft

To buy or sell, seen in the meaning and usage of the word when the book of Revelation was translated to English, is saying that you will not have a successful way of life unless you choose this kingdom on earth and its practices. The practices revolve around monetary income, a successful career, or a path of success enabled by the system's architects. They achieve this by engineering a system on established rules, but where the rules oppose the laws of the kingdom of heaven, thus denying access to those who do not serve them the ability to buy or sell. Those who exhibit the qualities of this earthly kingdom are shown favour in all aspects.

> **Wickedness thrives with wickedness, and evil is comfortable with evil.**

2 Corinthian 6:14 (KJV)

Be ye not unequally yoked together with unbelievers: for what fellowship hath righteousness with unrighteousness? and what communion hath light with darkness?

Without the ability to buy or sell using the 16th-century definition, those who do not choose the mark of the beast cannot plot the course of their lives, living in any semblance of success in this world, since the entire kingdom disenfranchises anyone who steps outside the bounds using occupation and income.

One might assume that just going to work is not choosing the world, and this may well be the case; however, if you take part in their ungodly activities, no matter how small, you choose the world. If you break the instructions of God, then you join their kingdom.

If you decide to keep the instructions of God, you choose the kingdom of God and once you stand your ground, the likelihood of you losing your job and way of life skyrockets to the almost inevitable.

"Come out of her my people[60]", is to separate yourself from the Beast—the world and its doctrine. To separate yourself, you need to follow the tenets, instructions, or commandments of the kingdom of heaven.

Chapter 10

A king sent his messenger to another kingdom to deliver a message to its inhabitants. The messenger gave the message as instructed, proclaiming he came in the king's name, but the news caused much distress amongst the natives; they killed the messenger using the excuse that the messenger claimed himself to be the king and thus deserved to die for blasphemy.

But was it blasphemy? And what was the real reason they killed the messenger?

Since the messenger proclaimed he came in the king's name, shouldn't he then speak as if he were the king?

John 12:49 (KJV)

For I have not spoken of myself; but the Father which sent me, he gave me a commandment, what I should say, and what I should speak.

John 5:43 (KJV)

I am come in my **Father's name**, and ye receive me not: if another shall come in his own name, him ye will receive.

The Son of God came in the name of the Father, and in that name, he executed the given commandments. The words he says are not of himself—not from his own will, but from what the Father has told him to speak.

John 14:8-9 (KJV)

[8] Philip saith unto him, Lord, shew us the Father, and it sufficeth us.

[9] Jesus saith unto him, Have I been so long time with you, and yet hast thou not known me, Philip? he that hath seen me hath seen the Father; and how sayest thou then, Shew us the Father?

With each verse, the light emerges that "name" represents identity. To represent or come in the name of someone is to assume that person's identity in executing whatever instruction they gave to you.

1 Samuel 25:5 (KJV)

And David sent out ten young men, and David said unto the young men, Get you up to Carmel, and go to Nabal, and greet him in my **name**

1 Samuel 25:25 (KJV)

Let not my lord, I pray thee, regard this man of Belial, *even* Nabal: for as his **name** *is*, so *is* he; Nabal *is* his **name**, and folly *is* with him: but I thine handmaid saw not the young men of my lord, whom thou didst send.

1 Samuel 2:12 (KJV)

Now the sons of Eli *were* sons of Belial; they knew not the LORD.

2 Corinthians 6:15 (KJV)

And what concord hath Christ with Belial? or what part hath he that believeth with an infidel?

2 Chronicles 2:1 (KJV)

And Solomon determined to build an house for the **name** of the LORD, and an house for his kingdom.

Amos 9:12 (KJV)

The Mark of the Beast

That they may possess the remnant of Edom, and of all the heathen, which are called by my **name**, saith the LORD that doeth this.

The name represents under whose power and doctrine you subscribe—whose instructions you follow, and who is your master or leader. Speaking or acting in the name of someone is operating under that person's power, command, instructions, and identity.

Luke 6:46 (KJV)

And why call ye me, Lord, Lord, and do not the things which I say?

Matthew 12:21 (KJV)

And in his **name** shall the Gentiles trust.

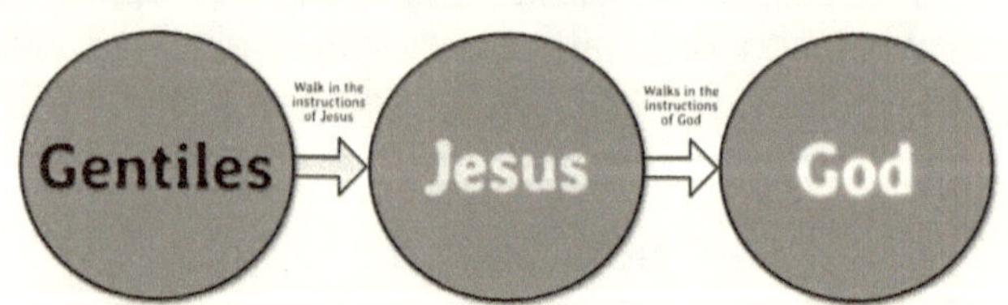

Therefore, the Gentiles walk in the instructions of God.

When speaking to the stranger, Manoah and his wife, the parents of Samson, enquired about his name (Judges 13:6[61], Judges 13:15-19[62]). They wanted to know who sent him and under what instructions he operates. Despite the question not being answered at the time of asking, we see the answer in Revelation 19:12-13[63]. The name of the stranger, Jesus, is the Word of God.

Many false teachers and false prophets[64, 65] come in the world's name, and so many people flock to them. Celebrities, scientists, educators, presidents and prime Ministers, preachers, religious leaders, YouTubers, influencers, etc. They tickle[66] the ears of the foolish, who are happy with the lies because it is what they want to hear; it's easier, satisfies the flesh, and doesn't require change and separation from the world. The lies enable laziness to thrive and mask wrong choices with fake justification while hiding the real reason. Fear!

When you serve this world in contrast to following the instructions of God, then you have the name of the beast—the kingdom which runs this world. When you do not operate under the teachings of the Son and transitively the Father—not man nor religion— you choose against the kingdom of God, this temporary kingdom on earth.

> The name is the identity, power, command, or instructions of who is your commander.

They killed the messenger because they wanted to continue operating in the name of the devil to serve themselves.

The Mark of the Beast

Chapter 11

The Number—666

Peter (2 Peter 2[67]) says that we will be made merchandise and how true this is. The single drive and obsession that is gripping this world is the ultimate measuring of everything in money for good or bad, success or failure:

- The ever-marching forward inflation and the desired effect of the rising prices of slavery.
- The structure of business and life where only profit matters—no matter how they get it.
- You are paying land taxes having already bought the land or property. You must question who owns the property and whether you were duped into buying something that will never belong to you.
- The monetisation of viewers, readers, subscribers with the ever-increasing ads and

platforms rewarding those publishers who never stop working—bondage.

- The mantra of consuming and having the best of everything, but never God.
- Another church collection-plate to save the foreign town or spread "the gospel", but somehow the church in the foreign village also collects to help another town somewhere else. Plus, nobody knows what the gospel is—do you?
- An avalanche of music and films pushes the abandonment of your soul by encouraging you to embrace the flesh and disregard the Spirit. The glorious prize of money dangles in front of your nose.
- And so much more.

Is greed good? What else does that one more magazine or television programme teach us? **Hate God, love money**.

Look around, including at yourself. See the disease, this obsession with money and worldly things that have gripped your body and those around you.

Is there nothing else to life? Is there nothing after death, or is it just reincarnation or a godless ascension to becoming a higher being?

Why is it okay to get "yours" at any cost? Even the pretence of nice is geared towards getting more money and the things of this world.

The instructions given to the kings of this kingdom are to be disciplined and show their love of God by keeping his laws to avoid corruption and ensure that the people they rule over can be close to God (Wisdom of Solomon 6:9-21[68]). Nobody follows, and the insidious underbelly fights nonstop[69] against the Ancient of Days[70]—God.

God draws us to him (John 6:37-44[71], Wisdom of Solomon 6:16[72]) and gives wisdom freely (James 1:5[73], Wisdom of Solomon 8:21[74], Wisdom of Solomon 9[75]) to those who ask.

There is always a condition: You must follow his instructions, operating in his NAME.

The Mark of the Beast

The Number of the Beast

Revelation 13:18 (KJV)

Here is wisdom. Let him that hath understanding count the number of the beast: for it is the number of a man; and his number *is* **Six hundred threescore *and* six**.

---

1 Kings 10:14 (KJV)

Now the weight of gold that came to Solomon in one year was **six hundred threescore and six** talents of gold

---

There are only three places in the scriptures that mention this number, and the third outside of the above two is 2 Chronicles 9:13, which is a chronicle of what is in the above **1 Kings 10:14**.

These verses show the connection between the number of the beast in Revelation 13 and the man. Solomon, in our eyes, was a great man and a righteous king; however, this is brought about by the teachings of Christianity, books and TV documentaries. In his later years, we know his wives caused him to stumble, but most of us do not know how many and the gravity of these mistakes.

Often, we make a mistake when reading or teaching the scriptures in assuming or giving the impression that every event is scripted to have a happy ending instead of just stating the facts. This misconception occurs because religions skew the understanding of the scriptures to agree with their doctrines foundations and increase their membership, and consequently, their income.

The fact is that Solomon broke (1 Kings 11:4-8[76]) many of the instructions (1 Kings 11:40[77], 1 Kings 12:2-4[78], Deuteronomy 17:15-17[79], Deuteronomy 7:3[80], Matthew 17:24-27[81]) given by God for kings and the layman.

- He married gentile women (Deuteronomy 7:3-4[82], 2 Corinthians 6:14[83]). Alliance or not, it does not matter; we must always follow the instructions of God.
- He multiplied wives to himself, marrying too many women (Deuteronomy 17:17[84]). How will he care for and satisfy all these women, but much more worrying is how will he guide all his children in the way of God?
- He multiplied horses (military power - 1 Kings 5:13-14[85]) using the men against God's instructions.
- He introduces taxes and burdens upon the people wherein (1 Kings 12:4[86], 2 Chronicles 10:4[87]) God has said the people should not

return to Egypt, the house of bondage—slavery (Exodus 20:1-3, Matthew 17:24-27). God told the Israelites via Samuel this would happen (1 Samuel 8:10-19), but they disregarded the warning.

- Add attempted murder to the list after God gave Jeroboam ten tribes of Israel to rule over because of Solomon's sins (1 Kings 11:40, 1 Kings 12:2-4).

- Solomon built places of rulership (high places—temples) for his wives where they ruled over the people and practised the customs of their respective gentile nations (Deuteronomy 17:15).

The priesthood is the highest place on earth where they stand as if God, doing the instructions of God; what a great sin Solomon committed here to have gentiles' rule over the people.

The Testaments of the Twelve Patriarchs - Judah - 21

"And now, my children, I command you, love Levi, that ye may abide, and exalt not yourselves against him, lest ye be utterly destroyed. For to me the Lord gave the kingdom, and to him the priesthood, and He set the kingdom beneath the priesthood. To me He gave the things upon the earth; to him

the things in the heavens. As the heaven is higher than the earth, so is the priesthood of God higher than the earthly kingdom, unless it falls away through sin from the Lord and is dominated by the earthly kingdom."

Book of Jasher 44:49-52

49. And she rose up and ascended to her temple in the house, and dressed herself in princely garments, and she placed upon her head precious stones of onyx stones, inlaid with silver and gold, and she beautified her face and skin with all sorts of women's purifying liquids, and she perfumed the temple and the house with cassia and frankincense, and she spread myrrh and aloes, and she afterward sat in the entrance of the temple, in the passage of the house, through which Joseph passed to do his work, and behold Joseph came from the field, and entered the house to do his master's work.

50. And he came to the place through which he had to pass, and he saw all the work of Zelicah and he turned back.

51. And Zelicah saw Joseph turning back from her, and she called out to him, saying What aileth thee Joseph? Come to thy work, and behold I will make room for thee until thou shalt have passed to thy seat.

> *52. And Joseph returned and came to the house, and passed from thence to the place of his seat, and sat down to do his master's work as usual and behold Zelicah came to him and stood before him in princely garments, and the scent from her clothes was spread to a distance.*

The Book of Jasher further highlights that a temple holds the seat of power. Zelicah sat at the entrance of Joseph's temple, where he sat on his seat of power to do his master's work.

- Solomon multiplied to himself silver and gold, which was against the instructions of God (Deuteronomy 17:17).

Solomon's father, David, instructed him to follow (1 Kings 2:1-4) the king of nations[88]—God, in everything he did. In the end, Solomon strayed from this way and followed the path of the heathens. This example signifies the world we see today and the love of money, wealth and the things of the world.

> The man referenced in Revelation 13 is Solomon. The number of talents of gold he required from the queen of the south was six hundred, threescore and six—666.

Matthew 12:42 (KJV)

The queen of the south shall rise up in the judgment with this generation, and shall condemn it: for she came from the uttermost parts of the earth to hear the wisdom of Solomon; and, behold, a greater than Solomon is here.

Jesus was indeed greater than Solomon and did not fall into the same trap that he did. He followed the instructions of God as opposed to Solomon and did not succumb to the flesh, the cares of this world and money. He did not put his trust in man but stayed faithful to God. Solomon's example when dealing with the queen of the south, the queen of Sheba, will be a testament against those who follow that road.

> She abandoned the things of the world and bought[89] the knowledge of God while Solomon left God for the things of this world.

Solomon's departure from God represents the number of the beast, succumbing to the love of money and the cares of this world.

> Greed is not good.

1 Timothy 6:10 (KJV)

For the love of money is the root of all evil: which while some coveted after, they have erred from the faith, and pierced themselves through with many sorrows.

Luke 21:34 (KJV)

And take heed to yourselves, lest at any time your hearts be overcharged with surfeiting, and drunkenness, and cares of this life, and so that day come upon you unawares.

Mark 4:15+19 (KJV)

---

15. And these are they by the way side, where the word is sown; but when they have heard, Satan cometh immediately, and taketh away the word that was sown in their hearts.

19. And the cares of this world, and the deceitfulness of riches, and the lusts of other things entering in, choke the word, and it becometh unfruitful.

Luke 8:14 (KJV)

And that which fell among thorns are they, which, when they have heard, go forth, and are choked with cares and riches and pleasures of this life, and bring no fruit to perfection.

Luke 17:26-28+32 (KJV)

---

26. And as it was in the days of Noe, so shall it be also in the days of the Son of man.

27. They did eat, they drank, they married wives, they were given in marriage, until the day that Noe entered into the ark, and the flood came, and destroyed them all.

28. Likewise also as it was in the days of Lot; they did eat, they drank, they bought, they sold, they planted, they builded;

32. Remember Lot's wife.

There are many people—**false prophets**, those who teach against the instructions of God whether in the church, the media, the government, the workplace, even your friends, relatives and neighbours who will try to trap you to follow their damnable heresies (2 Peter 2:1-4[90]). Do not walk with them (Proverbs 1:15[91]). Science, technology, and all their things cannot deliver them on that day of judgement (Zephaniah 1:18[92], 1 Timothy 6:20[93]).

Chapter 12

The Sum

The "mark of the beast" boils down to who you worship in thoughts and actions between God and this world. If you speak and do the acts of God, if you represent him, then you have the seal of God.

If you do and teach the things of this world, then you have the mark of this world and, by definition, the mark of the beast.

Revelation 9:4 (KJV)

And it was commanded them that they should not hurt the grass of the earth, neither any green thing, neither any tree; but only those men which have not the seal of God in their foreheads.

2 Timothy 2:19 (ESV)

But God's firm foundation stands, bearing this seal: "The Lord knows those who are his," and, "Let everyone who names the name of the Lord depart from iniquity."

You are what you eat, and whatever you ingest will be a testimony or evidence of who you are.

It's as simple as that!

To avoid the mark, you must do and teach the things of God; serve God by following his instructions and not this world or your flesh.

To find out the things of God, this is where you go to church, right?

No! Not.

The Mark of the Beast

> The stink of sin permeates the walls of those buildings and flows through the veins of its flock. Religion is a harlot that spreads its doctrine, which is cleverly intertwined with the world while spouting fairy tale boogeymen and persecution to control its congregations. At the same time, it fleeces them of all their wealth, time, expertise and honour[94].

God and his word must direct you and not others who trap you in the comfort of institutions serving themselves. At this time, you open his word and learn what he has said and trust in him and do the things you study.

Just as this world requires your entire life—your entire existence invested into it either through work, entertainment, influencing, control, politics, war, fighting or simply apathy, so does God require your whole life.

> **There are two kingdoms where you must join one or the other.**
>
> **There is no middle ground.**
>
> **Both require total commitment and no looking back.**

Revelation 3:16 (KJV)

So then because thou art lukewarm, and neither cold nor hot, I will spue thee out of my mouth.

Luke 9:62 (KJV)

And Jesus said unto him, No man, having put his hand to the plough, and looking back, is fit for the kingdom of God.

Chapter 13

Guidance

Examine the doctrines, and you see that the instructions given by God create a fair world where we all live together in harmony without war and suffering. Examine deeper, and you will see that is just the beginning.

Understand him before criticising out of ignorance.

If the people had time to reflect, would they surmise that there must be more to life than what is currently on offer? Without the tsunami of distraction and filth parading the world, would the Spirit of God in them guide them to the Most High God?

Inevitably, the Spirit will lead you to God; therefore, the distractions and the exploitation of the flesh are necessary for the beast. Without these things, this kingdom would fall like dominoes.

My words cannot quantify the monumental struggle we are in, so I refer to scripture.

Revelation 12:12 (KJV)

Therefore rejoice, *ye* heavens, and ye that dwell in them. Woe to the inhabiters of the earth and of the sea! for the devil is come down unto you, having great wrath, because he knoweth that he hath but a short time.

Understanding God and his righteousness clearly distinguish this world (kingdom—beast) we live in from the kingdom described in his word; his kingdom, if only to name one point, doesn't subscribe to slavery despite many claims. The accuser has enslaved the minds and bodies of the people, where they operate their daily lives as drones, chained to hedonistic debt, without realising it.

Our purpose here on earth is one-fold. We must put our efforts and faith (complete trust) in God and fight for the kingdom where we subscribe (Joshua 24:14-15[95]). The ones who ally with this world fight relentlessly for their domain; each of us, by following the instructions of Jesus, will fight for the kingdom of heaven.

The Mark of the Beast

33. Hear instruction, and be wise, and refuse it not.

34. Blessed is the man that heareth me, watching daily at my gates, waiting at the posts of my doors.

35. For whoso findeth me findeth life, and shall obtain favour of the LORD.

36. But he that sinneth against me wrongeth his own soul: all they that hate me love death.

We cannot serve God and money or the things of this world. We must live in this world for a short time until all the righteous people, past, present, and future, are prepared and harvested *(Some of us understand that the harvest is the end of the world[96], but looking deeper, the end of the world is when you die[97]. Your choice is made by how you live your life).* In this time, we must show our character and declare our allegiance, whether it be the world or God.

2 Esdras 5:42-48 (RSV)

42. He said to me, "I shall liken my judgment to a circle; just as for those who are last there is no slowness, so for those who are first there is no haste."

43. Then I answered and said, "Couldst thou not have created at one time **those who have been and those who are and those who will be**, that thou mightest show thy judgment the sooner?"

44. He replied to me and said, "The creation cannot make more haste than the Creator, neither can the world hold at one time those who have been created in it."

45. And I said, "How hast thou said to thy servant that thou wilt certainly give life at one time to thy creation? If therefore all creatures will live at one time and the creation will sustain them, it might even now be able to support all of them present at one time."

46. He said to me, "Ask a woman's womb, and say to it, 'If you bear ten children, why one after another?' Request it therefore to produce ten at one time."

47. I said, "Of course it cannot, but only each in its own time."

48. He said to me, "Even so have I given the womb of the earth to those who from time to time are sown in it.

Matthew 6:19-21 (KJV)

---

19. Lay not up for yourselves treasures upon earth, where moth and rust doth corrupt, and where thieves break through and steal:

20. But lay up for yourselves treasures in heaven, where neither moth nor rust doth corrupt, and where thieves do not break through nor steal:

The Mark of the Beast

21. For where your treasure is, there will your heart be also.

I can testify that God's promises are real, and his word is true. Do not fall for the lies of this world.

You will know the deceivers by their fruits.

Those who have the testimony of Jesus, **worship God**, will overcome this world, and despite being ridiculed and persecuted, their rewards will be great (Matthew 5:12[98], James 1:12[99], Matthew 16:27[100], Revelation 22:12[101], Revelation 2:10[102], Revelation 21:4[103], Jeremiah 17:10[104], Daniel 12:3[105], Isaiah 40:10[106]).

There will be difficulties in this life; let nobody fool you and say your life will be like a bowl of cherries. Understand that spiritual wickedness[107] sends physical entities in this world to deceive everyone. They persecute those who escape the deception, trying to bring them back in line through fear and suffering.

Let go of the world, your aspirations, property, career, pursuit of money, lifestyle, and desires. I do not say to give your assets to the church or charities, neither do I say to hold on to them, but what I say is your desires in this life must not be towards those things but to God. Be like a wise man, and after hearing the words of God, do them.

John 16:33 (KJV)

These things I have spoken unto you, that in me ye might have peace. In the world ye shall have tribulation: but be of good cheer; I have overcome the world.

Proverbs 28:26 (KJV)

He that trusteth in his own heart is a fool: but whoso walketh wisely, he shall be delivered.

Revelation 12:11 (KJV)

And they overcame him by the blood of the Lamb, and by the word of their testimony; and they loved not their lives unto the death.

Put your confidence in God and follow HIS instructions. Do not follow the instructions of men who profess to know God; get to know God for yourself through his teachings and not by what anyone tells you. Do the work yourself. Open the books and humble yourself.

Psalms 146:3 (KJV)

The Mark of the Beast

Put not your trust in princes, *nor* in the son of man, in whom *there is* no help.

Matthew 10:17 (KJV)

But beware of men: for they will deliver you up to the councils, and they will scourge you in their synagogues

---

Jeremiah 17:5-6 (KJV)

---

[5] Thus saith the LORD; Cursed *be* the man that trusteth in man, and maketh flesh his arm, and whose heart departeth from the LORD.

[6] For he shall be like the heath in the desert, and shall not see when good cometh; but shall inhabit the parched places in the wilderness, *in* a salt land and not inhabited.

There are consequences for not serving this world. You cannot buy or sell, and the world will persecute you. The result of not serving God is death. This fate, of course, is not physical death or the removal of your being from every existence, but as described in the following passage.

Revelation 14:9-11 (KJV)

---

[9] And the third angel followed them, saying with a loud voice, If any man worship the beast and his

image, and receive his mark in his forehead, or in his hand,

10. The same shall drink of the wine of the wrath of God, which is poured out without mixture into the cup of his indignation; and he shall be tormented with fire and brimstone in the presence of the holy angels, and in the presence of the Lamb:

11. And the smoke of their torment ascendeth up for ever and ever: and they have no rest day nor night, who worship the beast and his image, and whosoever receiveth the mark of his name.

Your actions in your life will judge you. Flip-flopping is not acceptable; deathbed confessions are not a real thing, so you must dedicate your life to one of these two kingdoms.

Excerpt from chapter 17, The Apocalypse of Paul (The judgement of an unrighteous man)

And the Lord God the righteous judge said: I say unto thee, O angel, I desire not of thee the account since it began to be fifteen years old; but declare its sins of five years before that it died and came hither. And again God the righteous judge said: For by myself I swear, and by mine holy angels and by my power, that if it had repented five years before it died, even for the walk (conversation) of one year, there should be forgetfulness of all the evil which it committed before and it should have pardon and remission of sins: but now let it perish.

Choose today whom you will serve.

Chapter 14
The Final Word

The end will come when all the past, present, and future servants of God are prepared and harvested—when there are no more righteous people in the world and none to come.

The example of final destruction is repeated throughout the scriptures; when there is a complete acceptance and indulgence in Sin, the world (earth, nation, city, or people) is destroyed:

- The flood in the days of Noah (Genesis 7 & 8).
- Sodom and Gomorrah's destruction (Genesis 19:24-25[108]).
- The destruction of the tribe of Benjamin, with only a few spared to save one tribe of Israel (Judges 20).

- The destruction of Canaan (Deuteronomy 9:5[109], Deuteronomy 7:1-2[110]) once there were no more righteous (Genesis 15:16[111]).
- And last, the prophecy of the return of God, as in the days of Noah (Matthew 24:37[112]).

So, what do you do?

Ecclesiastes 12:13-14 (KJV)

[13] Let us hear the conclusion of the whole matter: Fear God, and keep his commandments: for this is the whole duty of man.

[14] For God shall bring every work into judgment, with every secret thing, whether it be good, or whether it be evil.

References

---

[1] All the works inspired by God and not just the protestant Christian Bible.

[2] King of Kings – Another name for God.

[3] Isaiah 28:9-10 – [9] Whom shall he teach knowledge? and whom shall he make to understand doctrine? *them that are* weaned from the milk, *and* drawn from the breasts.
[10] For precept *must be* upon precept, precept upon precept; line upon line, line upon line; here a little, *and* there a little:

[4] Revelation 14:9-11 – [9] And the third angel followed them, saying with a loud voice, If any man worship the beast and his image, and receive *his* mark in his forehead, or in his hand, [10] The same shall drink of the wine of the wrath of God, which is poured out without mixture into the cup of his indignation; and he shall be tormented with fire and brimstone in the presence of the holy angels, and in the presence of the Lamb: [11] And the smoke of their torment ascendeth up for ever and ever: and they have no rest day nor night, who worship the beast and his image, and whosoever receiveth the mark of his name.

[5] Revelation 16:2 – And the first went, and poured out his vial upon the earth; and there fell a noisome and grievous sore upon the men which had the mark of the beast, and *upon* them which worshipped his image.

[6] Revelation 19:20 – And the beast was taken, and with him the false prophet that wrought miracles before him, with which he deceived them that had received the mark of the beast, and them that worshipped his image.

These both were cast alive into a lake of fire burning with brimstone.

7 Revelation 20:4 – And I saw thrones, and they sat upon them, and judgment was given unto them: and *I saw* the souls of them that were beheaded for the witness of Jesus, and for the word of God, and which had not worshipped the beast, neither his image, neither had received *his* mark upon their foreheads, or in their hands; and they lived and reigned with Christ a thousand years.

8 James 1:12 – Blessed *is* the man that endureth temptation: for when he is tried, he shall receive the crown of life, which the Lord hath promised to them that love him.

9 Matthew 25:21 – His lord said unto him, Well done, *thou* good and faithful servant: thou hast been faithful over a few things, I will make thee ruler over many things: enter thou into the joy of thy lord.

10 Revelation 22:12 – And, behold, I come quickly; and my reward *is* with me, to give every man according as his work shall be.

11 Jeremiah 17:9-10 – **9.** The heart *is* deceitful above all *things*, and desperately wicked: who can know it? **10.** I the LORD search the heart, *I* try the reins, even to give every man according to his ways, *and* according to the fruit of his doings.

12 2 Peter 2:1-3 – **1.** But there were false prophets also among the people, even as there shall be false teachers among you, who privily shall bring in damnable heresies, even denying the Lord that bought them, and bring upon themselves swift destruction. **2.** And many shall follow their pernicious ways; by reason of whom the way of truth shall be evil spoken of. **3.** And through covetousness shall they with feigned words make

merchandise of you: whose judgment now of a long time lingereth not, and their damnation slumbereth not.
13 Wisdom of Solomon 15:12 – But they counted our life a pastime, and our time here a market for gain: for, say they, we must be getting every way, though it be by evil means.
14 John 1:9 – *That* was the true Light, which lighteth every man that cometh into the world.
15 Matthew 13:12 – For whosoever hath, to him shall be given, and he shall have more abundance: but whosoever hath not, from him shall be taken away even that he hath.
16 Mark 3:24 – And if a kingdom be divided against itself, that kingdom cannot stand.
17 Matthew 13:10-11 – **10.** And the disciples came, and said unto him, Why speakest thou unto them in parables? **11.** He answered and said unto them, Because it is given unto you to know the mysteries of the kingdom of heaven, but to them it is not given.
18 Isaiah 55:8-9 – **8.** For my thoughts *are* not your thoughts, neither *are* your ways my ways, saith the LORD. **9.** For *as* the heavens are higher than the earth, so are my ways higher than your ways, and my thoughts than your thoughts.
19 Proverbs 16:16 – How much better *is it* to get wisdom than gold! and to get understanding rather to be chosen than silver!
20 Ecclesiastes 12:13-14 – **13.** Let us hear the conclusion of the whole matter: Fear God, and keep his commandments: for this *is* the whole *duty* of man. **14.** For God shall bring every work into judgment, with every secret thing, whether *it be* good, or whether *it be* evil.

---

[21] **Avalon** (/ˈævələn/; Latin: *Insula Avallonis*, Welsh: *Ynys Afallon, Ynys Afallach*; Cornish: *Enys Avalow*, literally meaning "the isle of fruit [or apple] trees"; sometimes written **Avallon** or **Avilion**).

[22] 1 Corinthians 3:19 – For the wisdom of this world is foolishness with God. For it is written, He taketh the wise in their own craftiness.

[23] Revelation 12:4 – And his tail drew the third part of the stars of heaven, and did cast them to the earth: and the dragon stood before the woman which was ready to be delivered, for to devour her child as soon as it was born.

[24] 2 Esdras 16:75 – Be ye not afraid neither doubt; for God is your guide

[25] Jeremiah 3:9 – And it came to pass through the lightness of her whoredom, that she defiled the land, and committed adultery with stones and with stocks.

[26] Jeremiah 10:8 – But they are altogether brutish and foolish: the stock *is* a doctrine of vanities.

[27] Ecclesiastes 1:14 – I have seen all the works that are done under the sun; and, behold, all *is* vanity and vexation of spirit.

[28] Ecclesiastes 12:13 – Let us hear the conclusion of the whole matter: Fear God, and keep his commandments: for this *is* the whole *duty* of man.

[29] Ecclesiastes 11:1-2 – [1.] Cast thy bread upon the waters: for thou shalt find it after many days. [2.] Give a portion to seven, and also to eight; for thou knowest not what evil shall be upon the earth.

[30] Revelation 17:15 – And he saith unto me, The waters which thou sawest, where the whore sitteth, are peoples, and multitudes, and nations, and tongues.

---

31 Proverbs 30:8 – Remove far from me vanity and lies: give me neither poverty nor riches; feed me with food convenient for me

32 Amos 8:11 – Behold, the days come, saith the Lord GOD, that I will send a famine in the land, not a famine of bread, nor a thirst for water, but of hearing the words of the LORD

33 Revelation 12:12 – Therefore rejoice, *ye* heavens, and ye that dwell in them. Woe to the inhabiters of the earth and of the sea! for the devil is come down unto you, having great wrath, because he knoweth that he hath but a short time.

34 Genesis 1:10 – And God called the dry *land* Earth; and the gathering together of the waters called he Seas; and God saw that *it was* good.

35 Matthew 16:18 – **16.** And Simon Peter answered and said, Thou art the Christ, the Son of the living God. **17.** And Jesus answered and said unto him, Blessed art thou, Simon Bar-jona: for flesh and blood hath not revealed it unto thee, but my Father which is in heaven. **18.** And I say also unto thee, That thou art Peter, and upon this rock I will build my church; and the gates of hell shall not prevail against it.

36 2 Timothy 3:16-17 – **16.** All scripture *is* given by inspiration of God, and *is* profitable for doctrine, for reproof, for correction, for instruction in righteousness: **17.** That the man of God may be perfect, throughly furnished unto all good works.

37 Isaiah 6:9 – And he said, Go, and tell this people, Hear ye indeed, but understand not; and see ye indeed, but perceive not.

38 Matthew 4:3-7 – **3.** And when the tempter came to him, he said, If thou be the Son of God, command that these stones be made bread. **4.** But he answered and said, It is written, Man shall not live by bread alone, but by every word that proceedeth out of the mouth of God. **5.** Then the devil taketh him up into the holy city, and setteth him on a pinnacle of the temple, **6.** And saith unto him, If thou be the Son of God, cast thyself down: for it is written, He shall give his angels charge concerning thee: and in *their* hands they shall bear thee up, lest at any time thou dash thy foot against a stone. **7.** Jesus said unto him, It is written again, Thou shalt not tempt the Lord thy God.

39 Proverbs 9:8-10 — **8.** Reprove not a scorner, lest he hate thee: rebuke a wise man, and he will love thee. **9.** Give *instruction* to a wise *man*, and he will be yet wiser: teach a just *man*, and he will increase in learning. **10.** The fear of the LORD *is* the beginning of wisdom: and the knowledge of the holy *is* understanding.

40 Matthew 12:25 — And Jesus knew their thoughts, and said unto them, Every kingdom divided against itself is brought to desolation; and every city or house divided against itself shall not stand:

41 Wisdom of Solomon 8:21 — Nevertheless, when I perceived that I could not otherwise obtain her, except God gave her me; and that was a point of wisdom also to know whose gift she was; I prayed unto the Lord, and besought him, and with my whole heart I said

42 James 1:27 — Pure religion and undefiled before God and the Father is this, To visit the fatherless and widows in their affliction, *and* to keep himself unspotted from the world.

43 Isaiah 28:9-10 — **9.** Whom shall he teach knowledge? and whom shall he make to understand doctrine? them that are weaned from the milk, and drawn from the breasts. **10.** For precept must be upon precept, precept upon precept; line upon line, line upon line; here a little, and there a little:

---

44 Luke 22:42 — **Saying,** Father, if thou be willing, remove this cup from me: nevertheless not my will, but thine, be done.

45 Revelation 19:10 — And I fell at his feet to worship him. And he said unto me, See *thou do it* not: I am thy fellowservant, and of thy brethren that have the testimony of Jesus: worship God: for the testimony of Jesus is the spirit of prophecy.

46 Romans 8:8-9 — **8.** So then they that are in the flesh cannot please God. **9.** But ye are not in the flesh, but in the Spirit, if so be that the Spirit of God dwell in you. Now if any man have not the Spirit of Christ, he is none of his.

47 Matthew 11:13 — For all the prophets and the law prophesied until John.

48 2 Thessalonians 2:1-10 — **1.** Now we beseech you, brethren, by the coming of our Lord Jesus Christ, and *by* our gathering together unto him, **2.** That ye be not soon shaken in mind, or be troubled, neither by spirit, nor by word, nor by letter as from us, as that the day of Christ is at hand. **3.** Let no man deceive you by any means: for *that day shall not come*, except there come a falling away first, and that man of sin be revealed, the son of perdition; **4.** Who opposeth and exalteth himself above all that is called God, or that is worshipped; so that he as God sitteth in the temple of God, shewing himself that he is God. **5.** Remember ye not, that, when I was yet with you, I told you these things? **6.** And now ye know what withholdeth that he might be revealed in his time. **7.** For the mystery of iniquity doth already work: only he who now letteth *will let*, until he be taken out of the way. **8.** And then shall that Wicked be revealed, whom the Lord shall consume with the spirit of his mouth, and shall destroy with the brightness of his coming: **9.** *Even him*, whose coming is after the working of Satan with all power and signs and lying wonders, [10.] And with all deceivableness of unrighteousness in them that perish; because they received not the love of the truth, that they might be saved.

[49] 1 Corinthians 3:16-17 — [16.] Know ye not that ye are the temple of God, and *that* the Spirit of God dwelleth in you? [17.] If any man defile the temple of God, him shall God destroy; for the temple of God is holy, which *temple* ye are.

[50] 1 Corinthians 6:15-20 — [15.] Know ye not that your bodies are the members of Christ? shall I then take the members of Christ, and make *them* the members of an harlot? God forbid. [16.] What? know ye not that he which is joined to an harlot is one body? for two, saith he, shall be one flesh. [17.] But he that is joined unto the Lord is one spirit. [18.] Flee fornication. Every sin that a man doeth is without the body; but he that committeth fornication sinneth against his own body. [19.] What? know ye not that your body is the temple of the Holy Ghost *which is* in you, which ye have of God, and ye are not your own? [20.] For ye are bought with a price: therefore glorify God in your body, and in your spirit, which are God's.

[51] Matthew 24:2 — And Jesus said unto them, See ye not all these things? verily I say unto you, There shall not be left here one stone upon another, that shall not be thrown down.

[52] John 4:21-23 — [21.] Jesus saith unto her, Woman, believe me, the hour cometh, when ye shall neither in this mountain, nor yet at Jerusalem, worship the Father. [22.] Ye worship ye know not what: we know what we worship: for salvation is of the Jews. [23.] But the hour cometh, and now is, when the true worshippers shall worship the Father in spirit and in truth: for the Father seeketh such to worship him.

---

53 Ezekiel 44:7 – In that ye have brought *into my sanctuary* strangers, uncircumcised in heart, and uncircumcised in flesh, to be in my sanctuary, to pollute it, *even* my house, when ye offer my bread, the fat and the blood, and they have broken my covenant because of all your abominations.

54 Ezekiel 44:9 – Thus saith the Lord GOD; No stranger, uncircumcised in heart, nor uncircumcised in flesh, shall enter into my sanctuary, of any stranger that *is* among the children of Israel.

55 Luke 24:44 – And he said unto them, These *are* the words which I spake unto you, while I was yet with you, that all things must be fulfilled, which were written in the law of Moses, and *in* the prophets, and *in* the psalms, concerning me.

56 Luke 18:19 – And Jesus said unto him, Why callest thou me good? none *is* good, save one, *that is*, God.

57 John 5:43 – I am come in my Father's name, and ye receive me not: if another shall come in his own name, him ye will receive.

58 Matthew 12:41-42 – **41.** The men of Nineveh shall rise in judgment with this generation, and shall condemn it: because they repented at the preaching of Jonas; and, behold, a greater than Jonas *is* here. **42.** The queen of the south shall rise up in the judgment with this generation, and shall condemn it: for she came from the uttermost parts of the earth to hear the wisdom of Solomon; and, behold, a greater than Solomon *is* here.

59 Luke 6:45 – **6.** And these words, which I command thee this day, shall be in thine heart: **7.** And thou shalt teach them diligently unto thy children, and shalt talk of them when thou sittest in thine house, and when thou walkest by the way, and when thou liest down, and when thou risest up. **8.** And thou shalt bind them for a sign upon thine hand, and they shall be as frontlets between thine eyes.

[60] Revelation 18:4 – And I heard another voice from heaven, saying, Come out of her, my people, that ye be not partakers of her sins, and that ye receive not of her plagues.

[61] Judges 13:6 – Then the woman came and told her husband, saying, A man of God came unto me, and his countenance *was* like the countenance of an angel of God, very terrible: but I asked him not whence he *was*, neither told he me his name:

[62] Judges 13:15-19 – [15.] And Manoah said unto the angel of the LORD, I pray thee, let us detain thee, until we shall have made ready a kid for thee. [16.] And the angel of the LORD said unto Manoah, Though thou detain me, I will not eat of thy bread: and if thou wilt offer a burnt offering, thou must offer it unto the LORD. For Manoah knew not that he *was* an angel of the LORD. [17.] And Manoah said unto the angel of the LORD, What *is* thy name, that when thy sayings come to pass we may do thee honour? [18.] And the angel of the LORD said unto him, Why askest thou thus after my name, seeing it *is* secret? [19.] So Manoah took a kid with a meat offering, and offered *it* upon a rock unto the LORD: and *the angel* did wondrously; and Manoah and his wife looked on.

[63] Revelation 19:12-13 – [12.] His eyes *were* as a flame of fire, and on his head *were* many crowns; and he had a name written, that no man knew, but he himself. [13.] And he *was* clothed with a vesture dipped in blood: and his name is called The Word of God.

[64] Matthew 7:15 – Beware of false prophets, which come to you in sheep's clothing, but inwardly they are ravening wolves.

---

65 Jeremiah 14:14 – Then the LORD said unto me, The prophets prophesy lies in my name: I sent them not, neither have I commanded them, neither spake unto them: they prophesy unto you a false vision and divination, and a thing of nought, and the deceit of their heart.

66 2 Timothy 4:3 – For the time will come when they will not endure sound doctrine; but after their own lusts shall they heap to themselves teachers, having itching ears;

67 2 Peter 2 – **1.** But there were false prophets also among the people, even as there shall be false teachers among you, who privily shall bring in damnable heresies, even denying the Lord that bought them, and bring upon themselves swift destruction. **2.** And many shall follow their pernicious ways; by reason of whom the way of truth shall be evil spoken of. **3.** And through covetousness shall they with feigned words make merchandise of you: whose judgment now of a long time lingereth not, and their damnation slumbereth not. **4.** For if God spared not the angels that sinned, but cast *them* down to hell, and delivered *them* into chains of darkness, to be reserved unto judgment; **5.** And spared not the old world, but saved Noah the eighth *person*, a preacher of righteousness, bringing in the flood upon the world of the ungodly; **6.** And turning the cities of Sodom and Gomorrha into ashes condemned *them* with an overthrow, making *them* an ensample unto those that after should live ungodly; **7.** And delivered just Lot, vexed with the filthy conversation of the wicked: **8.** (For that righteous man dwelling among them, in seeing and hearing, vexed *his* righteous soul from day to day with *their* unlawful deeds;) **9.** The Lord knoweth how to deliver the godly out of temptations, and to reserve the unjust unto the day of judgment to be punished: **10.** But chiefly them that walk after the flesh in the lust of uncleanness, and despise government. Presumptuous *are they*, selfwilled, they are not afraid to speak evil of dignities. **11.** Whereas angels, which are greater in power and might, bring not railing accusation against them before the Lord. **12.** But these, as natural brute beasts, made to be taken and destroyed, speak evil of the things that they understand not; and shall utterly perish in their own corruption; **13.** And shall receive the reward of unrighteousness, *as* they that count it pleasure to riot in the day time. Spots *they are* and blemishes, sporting themselves with their own deceivings while they feast with you; **14.** Having eyes full of adultery, and that cannot cease from sin; beguiling unstable souls: an heart they have exercised with covetous practices; cursed children: **15.** Which have forsaken the right way, and are gone astray, following the way of Balaam *the son* of Bosor, who loved the wages of unrighteousness; **16.** But was rebuked for his iniquity: the dumb ass speaking with man's voice forbad the madness of the prophet. **17.** These are wells without water, clouds that are carried with a tempest; to whom the mist of darkness is reserved for ever. **18.** For when they speak great swelling *words* of vanity, they allure through the lusts of the flesh, *through much* wantonness, those that were clean escaped from them who live in error. **19.** While they promise them liberty, they themselves are the servants of corruption: for of whom a man is overcome, of the same is he brought in bondage. **20.** For if after they have escaped the pollutions of the world through the knowledge of the Lord and Saviour Jesus Christ, they are again entangled therein, and overcome, the latter end is worse with them than the beginning. **21.** For it had been better for them not to have known the way of righteousness, than, after they have known *it,* to turn from the holy commandment delivered unto them.

The Mark of the Beast

---

22. But it is happened unto them according to the true proverb, The dog *is* turned to his own vomit again; and the sow that was washed to her wallowing in the mire.
68 Wisdom of Solomon 6:9-21 — **9.** Unto you therefore, O kings, do I speak, that ye may learn wisdom, and not fall away. **10.** For they that keep holiness holily shall be judged holy: and they that have learned such things shall find what to answer. **11.** Wherefore set your affection upon my words; desire them, and ye shall be instructed. **12.** Wisdom is glorious, and never fadeth away: yea, she is easily seen of them that love her, and found of such as seek her. **13.** She preventeth them that desire her, in making herself first known unto them. **14.** Whoso seeketh her early shall have no great travail: for he shall find her sitting at his doors. **15.** To think therefore upon her is perfection of wisdom: and whoso watcheth for her shall quickly be without care. **16.** For she goeth about seeking such as are worthy of her, sheweth herself favourably unto them in the ways, and meeteth them in every thought. **17.** For the very true beginning of her is the desire of discipline; and the care of discipline is love; **18.** And love is the keeping of her laws; and the giving heed unto her laws is the assurance of incorruption; **19.** And incorruption maketh us near unto God: **20.** Therefore the desire of wisdom bringeth to a kingdom. **21.** If your delight be then in thrones and sceptres, O ye kings of the people, honour wisdom, that ye may reign for evermore.
69 1 Maccabees 1:54-64 — **54.** Now the fifteenth day of the month Casleu, in the hundred forty and fifth year, they set up the abomination of desolation upon the altar, and builded idol altars throughout the cities of Juda on every side; **55.** And burnt incense at the doors of their houses, and in the streets.
56. And when they had rent in pieces the books of the law which they found, they burnt them with fire. **57.** And

whosoever was found with any the book of the testament, or if any committed to the law, the king's commandment was, that they should put him to death. **58.** Thus did they by their authority unto the Israelites every month, to as many as were found in the cities. **59.** Now the five and twentieth day of the month they did sacrifice upon the idol altar, which was upon the altar of God. **60.** At which time according to the commandment they put to death certain women, that had caused their children to be circumcised. **61.** And they hanged the infants about their necks, and rifled their houses, and slew them that had circumcised them. **62.** Howbeit many in Israel were fully resolved and confirmed in themselves not to eat any unclean thing. **63.** Wherefore they chose rather to die, that they might not be defiled with meats, and that they might not profane the holy covenant: so then they died. **64.** And there was very great wrath upon Israel.

70 Ancient of days – Another name for God.

71 John 6:37-44 – **37.** All that the Father giveth me shall come to me; and him that cometh to me I will in no wise cast out. **38.** For I came down from heaven, not to do mine own will, but the will of him that sent me. **39.** And this is the Father's will which hath sent me, that of all which he hath given me I should lose nothing, but should raise it up again at the last day. **40.** And this is the will of him that sent me, that every one which seeth the Son, and believeth on him, may have everlasting life: and I will raise him up at the last day. **41.** The Jews then murmured at him, because he said, I am the bread which came down from heaven. **42.** And they said, Is not this Jesus, the son of Joseph, whose father and mother we know? how is it then that he saith, I came down from heaven? **43.** Jesus therefore answered and said unto them, Murmur not among yourselves. **44.** No man

can come to me, except the Father which hath sent me draw him: and I will raise him up at the last day.
[72] Wisdom of Solomon 6:16 — For she goeth about seeking such as are worthy of her, sheweth herself favourably unto them in the ways, and meeteth them in every thought.
[73] James 1:5 — If any of you lack wisdom, let him ask of God, that giveth to all *men* liberally, and upbraideth not; and it shall be given him.
[74] Wisdom of Solomon 8:21 — Nevertheless, when I perceived that I could not otherwise obtain her, except God gave her me; and that was a point of wisdom also to know whose gift she was; I prayed unto the Lord, and besought him, and with my whole heart I said
[75] Wisdom of Solomon 9 — [1.] O God of my fathers, and Lord of mercy, who hast made all things with thy word, [2.] And ordained man through thy wisdom, that he should have dominion over the creatures which thou hast made, [3.] And order the world according to equity and righteousness, and execute judgment with an upright heart: [4.] Give me wisdom, that sitteth by thy throne; and reject me not from among thy children: [5.] For I thy servant and son of thine handmaid am a feeble person, and of a short time, and too young for the understanding of judgment and laws. [6.] For though a man be never so perfect among the children of men, yet if thy wisdom be not with him, he shall be nothing regarded. [7.] Thou hast chosen me to be a king of thy people, and a judge of thy sons and daughters: [8.] Thou hast commanded me to build a temple upon thy holy mount, and an altar in the city wherein thou dwellest, a resemblance of the holy tabernacle, which thou hast prepared from the beginning. [9.] And wisdom was with thee: which knoweth thy works, and was present when thou madest the world, and knew what was acceptable

in thy sight, and right in thy commandments. **10.** O send her out of thy holy heavens, and from the throne of thy glory, that being present she may labour with me, that I may know what is pleasing unto thee. **11.** For she knoweth and understandeth all things, and she shall lead me soberly in my doings, and preserve me in her power. **12.** So shall my works be acceptable, and then shall I judge thy people righteously, and be worthy to sit in my father's seat. **13.** For what man is he that can know the counsel of God? or who can think what the will of the Lord is? **14.** For the thoughts of mortal men are miserable, and our devices are but uncertain. **15.** For the corruptible body presseth down the soul, and the earthy tabernacle weigheth down the mind that museth upon many things. **16.** And hardly do we guess aright at things that are upon earth, and with labour do we find the things that are before us: but the things that are in heaven who hath searched out? **17.** And thy counsel who hath known, except thou give wisdom, and send thy Holy Spirit from above? **18.** For so the ways of them which lived on the earth were reformed, and men were taught the things that are pleasing unto thee, and were saved through wisdom.

76 1 Kings 11:4-8 — **4.** For it came to pass, when Solomon was old, *that* his wives turned away his heart after other gods: and his heart was not perfect with the LORD his God, as *was* the heart of David his father. **5.** For Solomon went after Ashtoreth the goddess of the Zidonians, and after Milcom the abomination of the Ammonites. **6.** And Solomon did evil in the sight of the LORD, and went not fully after the LORD, as *did* David his father. **7.** Then did Solomon build an high place for Chemosh, the abomination of Moab, in the hill that *is* before Jerusalem, and for Molech, the abomination of the children of Ammon. **8.** And likewise did he for all his strange wives, which burnt incense and sacrificed unto their gods.

77 1 Kings 11:40 – Solomon sought therefore to kill Jeroboam. And Jeroboam arose, and fled into Egypt, unto Shishak king of Egypt, and was in Egypt until the death of Solomon.

78 1 Kings 12:2-4 – **2.** And it came to pass, when Jeroboam the son of Nebat, who was yet in Egypt, heard *of it*, (for he was fled from the presence of king Solomon, and Jeroboam dwelt in Egypt;) **3.** That they sent and called him. And Jeroboam and all the congregation of Israel came, and spake unto Rehoboam, saying, **4.** Thy father made our yoke grievous: now therefore make thou the grievous service of thy father, and his heavy yoke which he put upon us, lighter, and we will serve thee.

79 Deuteronomy 17:15-17 – **15.** Thou shalt in any wise set *him* king over thee, whom the LORD thy God shall choose: *one* from among thy brethren shalt thou set king over thee: thou mayest not set a stranger over thee, which *is* not thy brother. **16.** But he shall not multiply horses to himself, nor cause the people to return to Egypt, to the end that he should multiply horses: forasmuch as the LORD hath said unto you, Ye shall henceforth return no more that way. **17.** Neither shall he multiply wives to himself, that his heart turn not away: neither shall he greatly multiply to himself silver and gold.

80 Deuteronomy 7:3 – Neither shalt thou make marriages with them; thy daughter thou shalt not give unto his son, nor his daughter shalt thou take unto thy son.

81 Matthew 17:24-27 – **24.** And when they were come to Capernaum, they that received tribute *money* came to Peter, and said, Doth not your master pay tribute? **25.** He saith, Yes. And when he was come into the house, Jesus prevented him, saying, What thinkest thou, Simon? of whom do the kings of the earth take custom or tribute? of their own children, or of strangers? **26.** Peter saith unto him, Of strangers. Jesus saith unto him, Then are the children free. **27.** Notwithstanding, lest we should offend them, go thou to the sea, and cast an hook, and take up the fish that first cometh up; and when thou hast opened his mouth, thou shalt find a piece of money: that take, and give unto them for me and thee.

82 Deuteronomy 7:3-4 — **3.** Neither shalt thou make marriages with them; thy daughter thou shalt not give unto his son, nor his daughter shalt thou take unto thy son. **4.** For they will turn away thy son from following me, that they may serve other gods: so will the anger of the LORD be kindled against you, and destroy thee suddenly.

83 2 Corinthians 6:14 — Be ye not unequally yoked together with unbelievers: for what fellowship hath righteousness with unrighteousness? and what communion hath light with darkness?

84 Deuteronomy 17:17 — Neither shall he multiply wives to himself, that his heart turn not away: neither shall he greatly multiply to himself silver and gold.

85 1 Kings 5:13-14 — **13.** And king Solomon raised a levy out of all Israel; and the levy was thirty thousand men. **14.** And he sent them to Lebanon, ten thousand a month by courses: a month they were in Lebanon, *and* two months at home: and Adoniram *was* over the levy.

86 1 Kings 12:4 — Thy father made our yoke grievous: now therefore make thou the grievous service of thy father, and his heavy yoke which he put upon us, lighter, and we will serve thee.

87 2 Chronicles 10:4 — Thy father made our yoke grievous: now therefore ease thou somewhat the grievous servitude of thy father, and his heavy yoke that he put upon us, and we will serve thee.

[88] King of Nation – Another name for God.

[89] Proverbs 23:23 – Buy the truth, and sell *it* not; *also* wisdom, and instruction, and understanding.

[90] 2 Peter 2:1-4 – [1.] But there were false prophets also among the people, even as there shall be false teachers among you, who privily shall bring in damnable heresies, even denying the Lord that bought them, and bring upon themselves swift destruction. [2.] And many shall follow their pernicious ways; by reason of whom the way of truth shall be evil spoken of. [3.] And through covetousness shall they with feigned words make merchandise of you: whose judgment now of a long time lingereth not, and their damnation slumbereth not. [4.] For if God spared not the angels that sinned, but cast *them* down to hell, and delivered *them* into chains of darkness, to be reserved unto judgment;

[91] Proverbs 1:15 – My son, walk not thou in the way with them; refrain thy foot from their path

[92] Zephaniah 1:18 – Neither their silver nor their gold shall be able to deliver them in the day of the LORD's wrath; but the whole land shall be devoured by the fire of his jealousy: for he shall make even a speedy riddance of all them that dwell in the land.

[93] 1 Timothy 6:20 – O Timothy, keep that which is committed to thy trust, avoiding profane *and* vain babblings, and oppositions of science falsely so called

[94] Proverbs 5 – [7.] Hear me now therefore, O ye children, and depart not from the words of my mouth. [8.] Remove thy way far from her, and come not nigh the door of her house: [9.] Lest thou give thine honour unto others, and thy years unto the cruel: [10.] Lest strangers be filled with thy wealth; and thy labours *be* in the house of a stranger;

---

95 Joshua 24:14-15 — **14.** Now therefore fear the LORD, and serve him in sincerity and in truth: and put away the gods which your fathers served on the other side of the flood, and in Egypt; and serve ye the LORD. **15.** And if it seem evil unto you to serve the LORD, choose you this day whom ye will serve; whether the gods which your fathers served that *were* on the other side of the flood, or the gods of the Amorites, in whose land ye dwell: but as for me and my house, we will serve the LORD.

96 Matthew 13:39 — The enemy that sowed them is the devil; the harvest is the end of the world; and the reapers are the angels.

97 The Apocalypse of Paul — And I when heard that sighed and wept, and said unto the angel: I would wait for the souls of the righteous and of the sinner, and see in what fashion they depart out of the body. And the angel answered and said unto me: Look again upon the earth. And I looked and saw the whole world: and men were as nought, and failing utterly; and I looked and saw a certain man about to die; and the angel said to me: He whom thou seest is righteous. And again I looked and saw all his works that he had done for the name of God, and all his desires which he remembered and which he remembered not, all of them stood before his face in the hour of necessity. And I saw that the righteous man had grown in righteousness, and found rest and confidence: and before he departed out of the world there stood by him holy angels, and also evil ones: and I saw them all; but the evil ones found no abode in him, but the holy ones had power over his soul and ruled it until it went out of the body.

98 Matthew 5:12 — Rejoice, and be exceeding glad: for great *is* your reward in heaven: for so persecuted they the prophets which were before you.

The Mark of the Beast

---

99 James 1:12 – Blessed *is* the man that endureth temptation: for when he is tried, he shall receive the crown of life, which the Lord hath promised to them that love him.

100 Matthew 16:27 – For the Son of man shall come in the glory of his Father with his angels; and then he shall reward every man according to his works.

101 Revelation 22:12 – And, behold, I come quickly; and my reward *is* with me, to give every man according as his work shall be.

102 Revelation 2:10 – Fear none of those things which thou shalt suffer: behold, the devil shall cast *some* of you into prison, that ye may be tried; and ye shall have tribulation ten days: be thou faithful unto death, and I will give thee a crown of life.

103 Revelation 21:4 – And God shall wipe away all tears from their eyes; and there shall be no more death, neither sorrow, nor crying, neither shall there be any more pain: for the former things are passed away.

104 Jeremiah 17:10 – I the LORD search the heart, *I* try the reins, even to give every man according to his ways, *and* according to the fruit of his doings.

105 Daniel 12:3 – And they that be wise shall shine as the brightness of the firmament; and they that turn many to righteousness as the stars for ever and ever.

106 Isaiah 40:10 – Behold, the Lord GOD will come with strong *hand*, and his arm shall rule for him: behold, his reward *is* with him, and his work before him.

107 Ephesians 6:12 – For we wrestle not against flesh and blood, but against principalities, against powers, against the rulers of the darkness of this world, against spiritual wickedness in high *places*.

108 Genesis 19:24-25 – **24** Then the LORD rained upon Sodom and upon Gomorrah brimstone and fire from the

LORD out of heaven; **25.** And he overthrew those cities, and all the plain, and all the inhabitants of the cities, and that which grew upon the ground.

109 Deuteronomy 9:5 – Not for thy righteousness, or for the uprightness of thine heart, dost though to possess their land: but for the wickedness of these nations the LORD thy God doth drive them out from before thee, and that he may perform the word which the LORD sware unto thy fathers Abraham, Isaac, and Jacob.

110 Deuteronomy 7:1-2 – **1.** When the LORD thy God shall bring thee into the land whither thou goest to possess it, and hath cast out many nations before thee, the Hittites, and the Girgashites, and the Amorites, and the Canaanites, and the Perizzites, and the Hivites, and the Jebusites, seven nations greater and mightier than thou; **2.** And when the LORD thy God shall deliver them before thee; thou shalt smite them, *and* utterly destroy then; thou shalt make no covenant with them, nor she mercy unto them:

111 Genesis 15:16 – But in the fourth generation they shall come hither again: for the iniquity of the Amorites is not yet full.

112 Matthew 24:37 – But as the days of Noe *were*, so shall also the coming of the Son of man be.

www.ingramcontent.com/pod-product-compliance
Lightning Source LLC
Chambersburg PA
CBHW021328060726
47591CB00006B/1930